PARENTING IN THE DIGITAL AGE

PARENTING IN THE DIGITAL AGE

T.J. RAVENSCROFT

CONTENTS

1. Introduction to Parenting in the Digital Age — 1
2. Understanding Technology and Child Development — 3
3. Balancing Screen Time and Other Activities — 7
4. Digital Safety and Online Etiquette — 11
5. Parental Controls and Monitoring Tools — 15
6. Tech-Savvy Parenting Strategies — 19
7. Building Healthy Tech Habits as a Family — 23
8. Navigating Social Media and Peer Influence — 27
9. Supporting Positive Online Relationships — 31
10. The Role of Schools and Educators in Digital Paren — 35
11. Parenting Styles and Their Influence on Tech Use — 39
12. Cultural and Socioeconomic Factors in Digital Pare — 43
13. Parental Self-Care and Digital Well-Being — 49
14. The Future of Parenting in a Tech-Driven World — 53
15. 15 — 57
16. Conclusion and Key Takeaways — 59

Copyright © 2024 by T.J. Ravenscroft
All rights reserved. No part of this book may be reproduced in any manner whatsoever without written permission except in the case of brief quotations embodied in critical articles and reviews.
First Printing, 2024

CHAPTER 1

Introduction to Parenting in the Digital Age

Parenting has never been an easy task. It gets even harder when the tools and toys kids love are the same ones that get them into trouble. This is why adults must be more vigilant than ever about what their children are doing online. As we'll see in the pages that follow, it's nearly impossible to provide firm figures about how many kids are exposed to the darker activities thriving in cyberspace, such as identity theft, identity abuse, and various forms of abuse. But it is painfully clear that many children are targets - some of the bad guys are professionals, specializing in stealing the identities of children, because they are blank slates, with no credit history to cause problems, while others are schoolmates, who often run afoul of technological advances that lead to fights, bullying, and the like.

Resolution of the difficulties is not as simple as saying "no" to the latest technologies (as we shall see later in this book, that battle was lost the moment parents started checking in with a four-year-old sitting in front of a computer monitor, playing games). However, other trends in technology, such as digital fingerprints, provide some protection that was not available a decade ago. Even so, parents have to be more aware of the dangers that face kids when they use digital technologies - without becoming so terrified of those dangers that they keep kids from learning useful skills that might be learned with the aid of emerging technologies.

Defining the Digital Age and Its Impact on Parenting
The Digital World is defined as the present technological era, starting in the 1980s and characterized by the digitization of information. At the simplest level, this is understood. But the Digital World is not just about the countless technologies like computers, mobile phones, the internet, and social media that have been (and continue to be) developed. Nor is it simply the quantity of digital information, the number of users, or the number of hours spent in the digital realm. These metrics quantify the effects of the Digital World, rather than describe its essence or the ways in which it has changed the human experience. The essence of the Digital World is the collection of opportunities—many seemingly boundless—brought about by the ability to digitize, store, process, and communicate not just information itself, but any form of human experience. This potential has influenced children's experience and upbringing in numerous ways.

Given the increasing influence of digital media on daily life, countless books, reports, articles, and websites exist on the topic of digital parenting. Here, the intention is not to confront any particular parenting theory or approach, but rather to consider the role and challenges of parenting in a tech-driven world, and its effects on children's health and happiness. Technology is here to stay. Parents have a duty to prepare their children for success in a digital future, making the best use of technology's benefits while guarding against harmful effects. In order to do so, they would be well-advised to take particular notice of children's mental health and well-being.

CHAPTER 2

Understanding Technology and Child Development

In the absence or disruption of these necessary frequent, intense, and emotion-laden interactions between parents and children, some children may face developmental and emotional difficulties. Difficulties could include learning, emotional, behavioral, and developmental challenges such as lower intelligence, obesity, language, social and emotional development problems, sleep disturbances, immune system problems, and stress, to name a few. Suboptimal conditions or traumatic situations could attract more serious developmental, behavioral, and emotional problems such as autism, anxiety disorders, depression, personality disorders, or psychosomatic adjustments with physical diseases such as irritable bowel syndrome.

Understanding how technology can affect your child's development is important. To do this, we must first be knowledgeable about the different aspects of the developing child. While children's experiences in their early years vary, the quality of their nurturing and relationships is a potent predictor of development and long-term health. Typically, children are largely dependent on their mothers or other primary caregivers for their nutritional, language, mental, and physical nourishment. For normal brain development, attention to the emotional and intellectual aspects of parenting is also important. Sensitive, responsive, interactive, and conversational engagement between parents and children makes the difference between poor and contributing brain/nervous system development.

Cognitive Development in the Digital Age

Children who are 2-7 years old are considered to be in the preoperational stage of cognitive development. The preoperational stage is characterized by the acquisition of knowledge of various subjects. At this stage, since the concept of learning through physical and verbal actions is effective among preoperational stage children, parents must utilize educational software applications that effectively develop their children's language, reading, writing, and arithmetic skills.

Cognitive development is divided into four stages of development that include sensorimotor, preoperational, concrete, and formal operational. These stages vary in time and content, with children aged 2 years old and below considered to be in the sensorimotor stage. In the sensorimotor stage, children acquire further knowledge about their day-to-day activities because of the gadgets used to stimulate the functioning of their different senses. At this stage, parents should expose their children to technology to stimulate the functioning of their different senses and develop better expression.

Social and Emotional Development in a Tech-Driven World

Most recently, kids have experienced and albeit limited but very immediate access to the virtual world. Raising emotionally-present kids ties in with the increasingly acute need to raise empathetic little beings with the ability to connect to others on a human, rather than purely technological, level. Although today's kids have greater access to potentially negative digital experiences than any previous cohort, they have also been given one absolute positive, which can shape the future of our planet and society at large.

At the same time, the unprecedented access to personal data by the wrong people (illegal hackers, or even established organizations who may influence the world or political events) can have a tremendous impact on all fronts of a person's or organization's life. So, in addition to imparting awareness about concepts and opportunities, parents need to make children understand the power, ethical use, and possibly the traps in technology, imparting both skill and integrity.

A related challenge for parents is to ensure that their children develop personal, social, moral, and character skills and values that technology cannot provide. Today's children have had access to any electronic device from an increasingly young age. Instant access to information has blessed them with more knowledge than any previous cohort, but without a corresponding emotional or social support system in the form of strong face-to-face interpersonal relationships, all that information may matter less.

Certainly, technology has made our world smaller by enabling people who are in different locations to interact with one another. For parents, this has meant a quicker means to building community and accessing information. In many cases, it is the only way they can connect with others, especially in times of staying home with young children. However, in the quest for connectivity and convenience, the danger exists of that connectedness and information access becoming a substitute for life in the real, physical world and a developing community.

CHAPTER 3

Balancing Screen Time and Other Activities

School work - allow screen time to be used for educational purposes. Friends - research shows that time spent on screens is replacing time spent with friends. Recreation - children also need time for any type of play (whether physical, imaginative, or creative) and active play. Family Time - screen time is replacing valuable family time as well. Dr. Rotbart says, "Screens often encourage walls to go up between family members so that they are sitting in the same room, but are all doing their own thing separately. Quality family time is incredibly important for a child's development and establishing connections for healthy relationships. Specifically, family meals together create opportunities for dialogue and emotional connections to be made."

To really understand how to balance screen time and other activities with your child, Dr. Rotbart suggests that you start by thinking about how your child is using the device. "If a child is using the device to talk to the grandparent who lives far away or if a child is using the device to research a school project," in both cases that's positive screen time. But if screen time is being used to replace other activities that are very important for your child's development, then that's when you should start asking some questions. Dr. Rotbart says when you start to think about those bigger questions, it's also worth noting the following:

Guidelines for Age-Appropriate Screen Time
Developing guidelines for age-appropriate media exposure requires understanding the different ways in which screens and their content affect children and teens at different developmental stages. Although the American Academy of Pediatrics (AAP) traditionally suggested a blanket "one hour of educational programming and co-viewing" rule for children over the age of two, a reappraisal and reevaluation of these guidelines is now taking place. This chapter discusses each stage of child and adolescent development. Age-appropriate screens have been discussed. However, if these guidelines are to emerge, either by AAP or another organization or coalition, it is crucial that they are created with input from those most affected: parents, educators, and pediatricians. Screen exposure should be delivered at the appropriate developmental limit for the child, and several considerations that differ by developmental stage should determine that exposure.

Promoting Physical Activities and Outdoor Play
Promote children's physical health. Play time is a crucial element for kids' growth. Time is necessary for physical development and for kids to increase their physical strength, increase balance and body coordination, and to develop fine motor skills. Activities are essential to stimulate kids' sensory development, to improve kids' mental and physical health, and to train self-regulation, imitation ability, and empathy. Stay close to nature. Offer kids a variety of choices to enjoy the pleasure of nature such as a big city garden with lots of vegetation for sufficient natural light and oxygen. Develop rela-

tionships with nature, allow children to have their own small garden and support them in resolving conflicts of nature foiling events. Give children the chance to send insects back to the woods and give earthworms a shower before going back to nature. Read more picture books and participate in outdoor activities with children to help them understand nature.

Limit screen time: The American Academy of Pediatrics recommends parents to limit screen time for young kids to a maximum of two hours a day and not to have any screen time 0-3 years old as the first 3 years is a time for brain development and social skill development. Create screen-free zones in and outside of the house. Parent role modeling behavior is very important. Being a good role model supports positive behavior and promotes use of screen time as a privilege for kids. It is a necessity to foster a balance between real and virtual life and for kids to model after their parent guardians. Another good habit to develop children's interest in their real surroundings is to encourage kids to play board games, to do family activities together and to participate in meaningful community service programs. Relieve stress, promote children's sense of mental and physical health, and encourage interactive and close parent-child relationships. As long as kids know that play time and screen time are not the same, it will help kids to realize that screen time should not take over their lives.

CHAPTER 4

Digital Safety and Online Etiquette

Aside from safety, another issue of extreme importance when it comes to your children using modern technology is the teaching of basic online etiquette and teaching morals and ethics conventions that differ in the rapidly growing technology sector. While many software companies and ISPs offer a digital safety tip sheet, email link, filtered search engines, and moderated conversations with kid-friendly content, it is important to instill your family's morals and ethics in their actions, including how to properly use online skills to complement their morals. Safer systems must be in place in households with children, acknowledging that many homes already allow children to use social networking sites and other phone, electronics, and software solutions that are becoming quickly integrated into children's daily interactions.

Your family's internet safety is of the utmost importance, especially because the technological world brings unanticipated risks that threaten children's safety. Once regularly connected to the internet for activities like games and homework, children gain access to chat and email. This means that children will have conversations with strangers, view adult material online if left unsupervised, or download material that could inadvertently expose the household to risqué material. To ensure that your children are safe from these possibilities, become familiar with filters and locks available through your phone, cell phone, ISP, and wireless devices and use them. Other safety controls available to parents and educators are cheap and easy to install; they include tools for monitoring and placing time limits on electronics.

Cybersecurity Measures for Children

Parents should regularly enforce media time-outs to ensure that children and teens take physical and mental breaks from the use of smart devices, and manage screen time and internet use by creating a digital schedule and teach kids how to be critical consumers of digital content. To monitor the activities, conduct and participation of children online, and keep them from engaging in inappropriate online discussions, using harmful apps, or cyberbullying, sextortion, and sexting, parents should be vigilant of their presence, operating times, and behavior in digital platforms and monitor usage logs, and install security software, antivirus and anti-malware protection when required.

As children are exposed to technology, it is important that cybersecurity measures are taken to ensure their safety online. To prevent their child from accessing unsuitable content online, parents can set up parental controls and website filtering software, router settings, and search engine settings customized for child-appropriate content. To safeguard private data and personal information such as the location of a child, parents should disable location services, Bluetooth, Wi-Fi, and GPS applications on the child's smartphone and restrict the sharing of information to strangers. Every digital platform that a child uses should have a unique and complex password that can be managed using password managers. Parents should only permit minors to use products, apps, and platforms that comply with privacy and security laws and regulations, and ensure that all software and devices are always kept up to date through the installation of security updates and patches.

Teaching Online Etiquette and Responsible Digital Citizenship

Be sure to mention the concept of "Internet Etiquette", otherwise known as "Netiquette", and teach your child other online manners that they are expected to follow. Discuss why. It is a good idea for the parents to know the Netiquette rules and how to present a positive digital reputation. With so many personalized and professional profiles, the internet has sometimes become the first impression maker. Providing real-world examples to show forever once uploaded doesn't mean first impression eraser might be helpful.

Use a serious yet respectful tone while discussing the legal and social consequences of negative comments, cyberbullying, catfishing, and sexual harassment. Because people are more likely to behave disrespectfully online than they would in real life, the legal consequences are surprising. The US Brighton laws prohibit cyberbullying and provide restitution to the victim for those who participate in creating a situation where the victim has to screen his calls and emails in order to feel safe. Several instances of internet-based relationships in the last few years, where a court awarded the deceived virtual lover with tens of thousands of dollars in damages, support catfishing's illegalities. Similarly, a local district attorney prosecuting a long-term case involving a minor who was asked to send nude pictures and felt there was no way out other than to comply discussed some unwittingly illegal underage or revenge porn.

CHAPTER 5

Parental Controls and Monitoring Tools

Following the extensive media coverage in 2017, more and more people are incorporating Internet of Things devices into their homes and lives. One important concern not to be overlooked: security and privacy. The State of European Consumers report revealed that 78% of consumers show great concern regarding how secure their data is, with 40% reporting worries that their data is not secure from hackers. As smart products continue to make their way into our homes, it is necessary to also make sure attached security systems and procedures are also 'smart' and offer bona fide protection.

The Internet of Things invites television, fridge, lighting, and other gadgets to hop online and get 'smart'. Through Wi-Fi or Bluetooth, they listen and talk to each other and to us. And they might also listen to people who they are not allowed to. Welcome the Z-Wave SmartThings Hub, the D-Link security camera, the Z-Wave front door lock, the smart baby monitor, and the LG Smart Fridge: just a selection of some Internet-of-Things devices that fall far behind the levels of protection we expect today.

Overview of Parental Control Software

Parental control software is an easy, persuasive answer for those parents who can't say no indefinitely, monitor every electronic device used and continuously oversee kids. The real question to ask is whether or not parental control software brings the solution; in reality, it could only be a deterrent. Educational tools for older children aren't much more than an electronic house arrest system, although they might discourage inappropriate invitation, false disclosure and malicious online practices. Young children can literally find themselves in mortal danger, and the tools can supply relevant protection. Studying these tools can give parents insights into the most hush-hush online activity of their kids – even when they're dealing with rebellious teens. When parents become concerned enough, parental control software will provide a watchful eye at the computer. In more extreme cases, it might form the basis of a home rehabilitation program against commercial addiction.

Parental control tools have traditionally come in three basic types: web blockers, which limit what is permissible and what is off-limits as far as web use is concerned; activity loggers, which can monitor what's being done, to include what kids are writing and their general computer usage; and computer time limiters, which control the amount of time a computer can be in use.

The topic of parental control (monitoring) software is a touchy area – at least for parents. For teenagers and children, the subject probably won't be nearly as contentious, or perhaps even as serious. Parental control software in its various forms differs in the way it is supposed to be implemented and function at the tech level; but its fundamental core is that it allows parents to keep track of what kids are doing while they're online.

How to Have Effective Conversations About Monitoring
Following the analogical parental talks, you can never be too safe when it comes to speaking with your kids about online safety and internet usage boundaries. Be sure to talk to your kids regularly about the proper and improper ways to use the internet. It may sound and feel like hammering your kids with loads of questions right now is productive, but the relative distance that you've established may serve to exacerbate your child's natural lack of forthrightness. You might find it beneficial to just be around as quietly as possible while they're on the computer, and give them some time to get comfortable with your presence. A mere dry run now can do wonders, soothing those social jitters and helping your talk run smoother in the future. Document as much as you can, any behaviors or problems that you spot. Be respectful of their privacy as much as you can. That helps establish trust without forcing someone to learn too much about themselves.

In order to promote a healthy dialogue about the internet and its associated risks, parents will need to create a comfort level in both themselves and their children. To facilitate ongoing conversations and effective parenting, the following conversations should be employed in a regular manner and as subject matter arises:

CHAPTER 6

Tech-Savvy Parenting Strategies

There is ample research to suggest that both the quantity and quality of parenting time matter for children's development. But all time is not equal, so a number of recommendations follow, ensuring that this time is productive and geared to cultivating talent, as much as it is about simply ensuring children are occupied while parents are working. Given that parental time is a scarce resource and digital technologies are increasingly distracting children and parents alike, it is important to remind parents to allocate their focus and attention wisely. A win-win would be to suggest that any time spent engaged with the family media diet should address the 'twin trilemmas' of screen time: overconsumption (quantity), improperly designed content (quality), and parentally-facilitated usage (monitoring), not only for children but for parents as well.

A nuanced approach to parenting is especially important in the digital age. Given that nearly all children now have platforms from which to amplify their voices, power structures in the family are shifting. At the same time, large corporations like Facebook and Google have ignited discussions about digital consumption, privacy, advertising, and the exploitation of personal information. While parenting norms are evolving—partly as a result of more kids having a broad range of digital and social experiences—the role incredibly influential tech companies play in children's lives must also be addressed.

Encouraging Critical Thinking and Media Literacy Skills

Digital technology is part of children's lives and it can have a positive impact on early learning. Any guidelines therefore need to focus on the child and be inclusive for all unique learning and communication styles. Today's parents and children interact with digital technologies from the first moments of life. However, the benefits of digital technology may vary at certain stages of children's development. The youngest need guidance to maximize the benefits of digital exposure and minimize risks through practical and supportive advice. At the same time, children from the age of two are generally more stimulated to learn using digital media, though their learning is significantly enhanced when supported by adult interactions. This is the age when recorded media, such as television, videos, and video games, can be used to support children's learning and development. Children under the age of 18 months are not ready for traditional screens and touching them gives them no real benefit. Instead, they learn best from face-to-face, 'back-and-forth' interactions. On the other hand, toddlers aged 18 months to 24 months can learn new words from using interactive touchscreens.

Today's youth grow up in a digitally saturated world, which significantly impacts the way our children learn, communicate, and play. While digital technologies offer a range of exciting opportunities, they also pose challenges and risks. For these reasons, children need an informed and constructive environment where they receive advice and support on how to navigate digital technologies safely, responsibly, and critically. As they grow, children will be increasingly faced with digital life challenges. Maximizing the benefits for children while minimizing the risks requires well-informed parents and trusted caregivers. Parents and caregivers play a crucial role in supporting their children's digital experiences by being actively involved in how their children engage with digital technologies. It is the first three years of life that make the biggest difference in a child's development while the first eight years of life set the stage for decades to come.

Setting Boundaries and Consistent Rules Around Technology Use
Every family is different, and so are use of technology rules. Rules around technology use might also require some negotiating. Your teenager might insist that homework time needs to include instant messaging capabilities, making the television or personal digital assistant an essential part of the homework equation. Using the computer might be non-negotiable for your writing-aspiring teen. Come up with a technology use policy based on the unique dynamics of your family and age of your kids. Setting a few consistent rules at the outset can help your child have a healthy relationship with technology. By placing appropriate limits, the entire family will start out with a clear understanding of how technology will be a healthy and fun part of everyday life. So work with your child to create a "flexible but consistent" daily agenda.

Some reminders here: "Eat your breakfast." "Don't forget to wear warm clothes today." "That's enough screen time for today." Yes, there is a rule around technology use! Prevent the dinner scene that we discussed earlier by setting boundaries and consistent rules around technology use. Set a regular time for technology use, just like any other activity. This could be just after dinner when all homework is complete, but before bedtime. Understanding the rules around technology in your home will prevent kids from trying to gain as much screen time as possible, and then trying to push the boundaries trying to obtain a few more minutes every day.

CHAPTER 7

Building Healthy Tech Habits as a Family

Tech education is happening at school, whether it's happening at home or not. As part of the gentle teaching strategy, build little digital check-ins and project heats. For something bigger, hold off a few moments until a quiet time, when the conversation can last and feels natural, and then experiment a bit more before saying no. Technology fluency is about feeling sensible and protected enough to self-assertively navigate and discover. Support being safe, wise choices. And model it for them. Provide opportunities to understand digital literacy by themselves, from other relatives, or for some reliable, guided guidance - and power. Remember, these moments of coaching are not about protecting them from everything - they're about showing them how to be clever and tough when you're not present. The most powerful option for keeping kids secure is the one sitting with them. mainScreen is active, casplockWithPath.

Tech behaviors are not just about limits - it's the quality of time and engagement that matters. We want to raise kids to be people - not just live as people. So talk about your concerns and hopes around technology use. But find the middle ground between digital reliance and avoidance. Some of us have different views which can be sources of family tension. That's fine. Come to a consensus in your home, then you can extend rules and norms within your community. While it's essential to stay on top and involve ourselves with kids' tech behavior, they need some distance. Sometimes invite them to teach you something new you can share together.

Creating Tech-Free Zones and Times in the House

Keep your gadgets in a central location and refrain from checking your phone all the time. Try to avoid using technology as a babysitter, giving yourself a break from your kids, getting very involved in your own online activities, or paying more attention to what's going on. Make sure you do not mirror bad behavior and check yourself when you feel the urge to use your gadgets too much. This includes not using your gadgets at the dinner table, during family conversations, while watching television or a movie as a family, or during game nights with the family. Communicate concerns to your children if they have been using too much technology and make sure that they know why you feel that way. Then, enforce reasonable limits on what they can do and when.

Then, there are still some things you can do to promote moderation and cut down on the negative effects of technology. One of the best things you can do to this end is to set up a technology-free zone and times in your house. This will be an area or time in which all members of the family (parents included) are not allowed to use any form of technology. You can reserve this for certain times of day if needed and even make it a family activity to encourage family bonding and discourage you from using your gadgets. Some suggestions for this time include during meal times, after school in the early evening, and first thing in the morning before the kids head off to school.

Engaging in Tech-Free Family Activities

For children to be able to make tech-free choices, it is necessary for parents to be aware of what tech-free activities are and the benefits of these activities. Tech-free family activities provide many bonding and positive skills that allow family members to become closer, express themselves more, experience less stress and enjoy life more. Children need to experience the feeling of being bored, so that they become resilient to the feeling of being bored. As a parent, helping your children experience boredom positively is a chance to help them develop important life skills that are beneficial now and into the future. By knowing what to do when they are bored, it reduces the number of negative consequences that could occur while having access to tech devices. Boredom can be good! And is a time that allows the body and mind to take a break. The mind uses this time to transform the boring time into something creative and meaningful and gives children a chance to engage in tech-free family activity.

Some families are really enjoying their tech-free activities and are starting to do more of them than ever before. Parents and kids are actually finding out that their kids are pretty neat company. Board games, as applicants mentioned, are a great way to have tech-free time. In fact, families are a lot more excited about game nights than they have been for a long time. Some other fun suggestions for tech-free engaging in tech-free family activities include: going outside as a family, going for a walk or bike ride, being part of a volunteer or service project, eating dinner as a family, going out for a meal, doing a craft or art project, being part of a sports game, exercise or physical activity as a family, and doing a fun educational activity like a trip to the museum, zoo, library or other creative educational adventure. Take some time and see what tech-free family activities your family can enjoy. You will find that it is very exciting and fun.

CHAPTER 8

Navigating Social Media and Peer Influence

When parents enroll their child in the journey through the digital jungle, they must act as tour guides, ensuring the excursion includes a map, compass, and history lessons in case the adventure goes awry. The rocky terrain found on the journey can include exposure to adult content, exploitation through predators, cyberstalking, and child pornography, and a moat filled with malicious intent, phishing, bullying, and fake websites, and even bombs or bullying via computer. We all play a critical role in educating children about how to make good decisions about their internet safety and digital wellness. The more a parent understands about the social networking world, the better prepared the child will be when encountered there.

The teenage years are when kids develop their identity. Along the way, kids may act impulsively and without a healthy dose of reality and internet wellness, the interesting pictures they paint of themselves may manifest long-term social and psychological consequences. A high level of stress is placed on looking good and getting likes that teens may be sacrificing their values without fully realizing. Not everything that looks good is good for us. Parents need to become informed about relevant research on positive youth development and peer relationships. By helping teens gain deeper self-knowledge and active appraisals of peers, parents promote insight that will facilitate self-regulation around technology and social media in particular. Teaching district beliefs and values are important. Help them see beyond the never-ending selfie.

Understanding the Impact of Social Media on Children and Teens
Quality communication skills are of utmost importance. For the younger generation, there are multiple technologies that are being used by children for most part of the day. However, these children are not necessarily communicating effectively through speech with the people surrounding them, like their classmates in the school, who are instead, also on their devices. Digital devices can affect social cues such as tone of voice and facial expression that help us create meaning, can interrupt our natural desire to empathize. If messages are not reinforced by some nonverbal facial and bodily cues, they can be misinterpreted or misperceived, or are open to interpretation. This can affect the way that people learn to understand the emotions of others, which is a vital foundation in developing empathy, and can also result in less effective communications with real people.

To understand the impact of social media (or any other technology) on young children or teens, we must understand the underlying processes through which social media exerts its effects. It is a complex interaction, made up of the interaction of biological, affective, psychological, social, and cultural factors. Of course, people of all ages can be affected by social media. But for children and teens, who have a more neuroplastic brain, are going through the sensitive periods of forming an identity, and are using technology as their main source of communication, these effects further expand. Some of the key issues, such as multitasking, addiction, effectiveness of social media communication in dealing with distress, and issues related to self-expression through the totally fabricated virtual reality are among the specific issues which are of importance to the young population.

Teaching Responsible Social Media Use

We do not provide funds directly for Facebook, YouTube, MySpace, or other social media platforms, which also monitor each child's activity (all of which provide a contract for what is appropriate on our part and theirs!). As avenues for negotiation, we let our kids know that we are always curious and always nearby, which ensures some measure of responsibility or moderation on both sides. We haven't had many problems. What addicting online hold social media might have is in this vein: as our kids text our office numbers when away from home again, they can reach us or be reached no matter where we are. It makes sense in a lot of ways. Still, social media is a powerful and influential tool, and it is a wise parent who does not take well-thought-out precautions for their responsible usage.

Social media is ubiquitous and has enormous influence, but it is also a great concern for parents. Will MySpace and Facebook profiles come back to haunt our kids later in life? Is stranger danger digital now, and is it something we can teach? The general rule we have for our kids and their virtual lives is the same we have for their actual lives, and that is to trust them until they give you a reason not to. That said, we also set certain technology guidelines and parameters early on, particularly about the permanence and observability of actions and comments online. But for the most part, we trust our daughters to do the right things and make the right choices. Technologies change, but people remain the same. Most girls are hardwired to be fussy about their mothers and strive for the approval of their fathers. They want to make us proud, in the same way we want them to make us proud.

CHAPTER 9

Supporting Positive Online Relationships

Children and teenagers' constant exposure to digital environments is quite recent, and our knowledge about how they relate digitally is still developing. Various researchers are working on this issue within the field of media studies, exploring the key features of peer digital cultures among primary and secondary school students. These cultures are now almost completely occupied by social networks – a series of Web 2.0 platforms that allow people to share materials, ideas, and information and execute specific actions, all of which involve direct social interaction. A part of these social platforms is created explicitly for adolescents and their social interaction. Despite somewhat age-related restrictions for many social network accounts (such as, for example, being 13 to have a Facebook profile), teenagers often find ways to avoid these restrictions and participate anyway in multiple social network interactions.

With the advances in technology, new opportunities for connection and new platforms for expression and communication may seem almost second nature for many adults. For some youth, technology may be the vehicle they use every day to create, communicate, socialize, and learn. New information and communication technology influence the social worlds of children and youth in important ways. They know the power of the internet from a young age because social networks are an integral part of many of their activities. These new interactions can provide both opportunities and risks for young people.

Encouraging Empathy and Kindness Online

Once your child is socially active in a digital community, you can be a coach, sitting with your child as he drafts his first comments. Remind him of the signs of a successful interaction, like thoughtful comments and shared experiences. Cite relevant examples, either positive or negative, from your own online interactions or those of friends and family. You can provide clear gems like "That's a thoughtful comment - I'd like to see more of that," or "That seemed a little pushy to me, especially when you kept repeating it." Your child will like the role of having his mother or father there, and having a knowing eye will help him avoid some embarrassment. Be sure to address negative peer pressure as it occurs, with email apologies and conversation about the right thing to have done instead.

From a young age, your child should naturally learn how to be kind to other people. Hopefully, you've led the way with "please" and "thank you" and asked, "What do you say?" when you know your child should be expressing gratitude. Building empathy and kindness into your family culture will carry over into your child's digital relationships. Because caring looks a bit different online, make sure to model positive interactions with your social media and texting. Especially when kids are in both physical and emotional conversations, they need strong adult role models of safe and kind interactions.

Dealing with Cyberbullying and Online Conflict
The bullying and racism and violence between young people seen particularly frequently in chat rooms are terrifying, whatever their causes. The bottom line is that every child being parented in digital times needs the guidance to question the motives behind every action online, whether it's her own or the interaction with others.

Most social networking sites have complex privacy settings that allow you to control who is able to see your or your child's personal information and what can be shared with others. You can, for example, select who can see your child's profile, who can contact her, and who can see the information she publishes. The level of privacy and security you choose also buckle up if it is enabled properly.

Ignoring online information doesn't work, so you need to report abusive behavior directly to your ISP or mobile phone operator as soon as possible. In addition, you or your kids should report offensive or inappropriate material to the website hosting the information. Once a child has received bullying messages, she needs to either block or delete the offender, and perhaps also block or report the person involved. Also, she or you can make sure that your mobile phone is set not to accept calls or messages from this source and then set up a new phone number to give to friends and family.

Explaining to your kids that the injection of technology doesn't give free rein to be a different person online is essential. Kids are often surprised at how quickly interactions can escalate, so need clear guidelines about what to do and when. They must not retaliate but must tell you immediately, and trust that you will not overreact unduly.

Dealing with bullies has been an age-old parenting challenge, but cyberbullying is a new and particularly troubling problem to negotiate. Online conflict can make a child feel physically threatened, and the feeling of no escape can result in extreme stress, anxiety, and depression. Technology in general and social networking in particular can foster such abusive behavior because of the impersonal nature of communication.

CHAPTER 10

The Role of Schools and Educators in Digital Paren

One potential role is for schools to host periodic family or parent technology nights where parents can gather to share knowledge, ask questions, and discuss current issues. Schools can provide curriculum for these events, giving parents an in-depth look at the types of digital safety messages kids are receiving at school (e.g., cyberbullying, responsible online behavior) and also provide parents with an opportunity to discuss learning activities that rely on technology use, introduce different devices and types of educational software available for children, as well as discuss the variety of resources to which students have access at school. Finally, schools can provide opportunities for parents to network with each other. These technology nights enable families with different levels of comfort with technology to talk about their thoughts, to learn from each other and to support each other in digital parenting matters.

There is great potential for schools and educators to significantly benefit parents in their digital parenting role as well as help address the growing gap between school and home digital technology usage. By playing an active role in digital safety training opportunities, schools can help parents learn and understand the safety features and other functions of digital devices and technology resources – resources that kids use and need for school as well as for fun. In addition, schools can lead by example and utilize consistent policies and practices at the school and district level to ensure families also focus on the most positive benefits technology has to offer.

Collaborating with Schools to Promote Digital Literacy

As schools struggle to fund computer replacements, parents might be able to donate usable home equipment to the cause. As kids formally study Internet search strategies, parents can help by passing along the basics of the search sequence, strategy, and criteria that can focus any child's Googling and cut the time necessary to find the material that they need. Eventually, each child even benefits when a parent expresses an interest in what has been learned - so kids study more and learn better. This reverse support of the children's online interests by both educators and parents, lessons bearing seeds of long-term at-home support, helps students learn to navigate the sea of information, limit class work to a reasonable duration, and - as a byproduct - enables parents to shield kids at home from inappropriate material.

Children spend many of their waking hours at school where a vast array of learning resources exist, delivered and presented by teachers and through web-based environments. Parents and schools collaborate to ensure that children are safe, respectful, and responsible citizens. Why, then, is digital literacy an exception? Rather than leave Internet resources unplumbed, consider working with the school and the school board to identify potential hazards as well as introducing kids to the right tools for research. This way, educators can provide a context that promotes the responsible, legal use of digital technology in educational projects. For example, educators might encourage students to download reference material for offline use so that they are not entirely dependent on erratic Internet access. Schools might schedule computer time during class for completion of homework or searches for pictures or videos needed for projects so that students avoid late-night holes at Disney.com or YouTube.

Incorporating Digital Citizenship into School Curricula

Some parents may feel a sense of inadequate authority over their children as they attempt to navigate the digital world. Educators have considerable influence over a child's social and emotional development. Students often adopt the common values of their school, providing an opportunity to instruct and reinforce proper online behavior. Incorporating digital citizenship discussions into the regular school curriculum can guide students on ethical and thoughtful behavior when using diverse forms of technology at home and in the classroom. Students must recognize that they share their learnings with others from all over the world who may not share the same perspective. Often, students and parents take for granted the idea of citizenship in a physical school setting, but doing so in a digital environment can be overlooked or not emphasized enough. Encouraging online collaborative projects and other types of electronic communications between classes can also allow students to utilize technology in a creative, engaging, and educationally productive manner.

CHAPTER 11

Parenting Styles and Their Influence on Tech Use

In fact, the social contexts in which children function, including the nature of the support they receive from home and school, the quality of relationships they have with their peers, and the ways media is used, suggest that we expand inquiries into child development. And, not only are we to ask about how media is used to reach social learning goals, but also ask what the technology does to child development when it is used as such. Since some questions have been addressed, we wondered if others might shed more light on actual child behavior. After all, what point is redefining what distinguishes collaborative behaviors if social media fails to induce such behavior? We began to move from questions of mere exposure to technology and kids and their stereotypic responses to how kids and technology interact. After all, kids are not inherently passive media consumers. They use media to become involved in meaningful activities and create something new. As children use various tools and media for participating in social (e.g. social media), cognitive (the ways they learn to function within a community), or psychological (how they construct their individual selves) activities, their burgeoning agency comes out to play. And, in doing so, they basically tell us they can create in one area but reinforce traditional conceptions of youth and media in others. We just didn't ask quite right.

Research on the effects of parenting on child technology use is limited, and setting rules is apparently the most frequently studied parenting variable. However, others must also come into play. That said, we do know a couple of things. Parental expectations of others are among the strongest influences on a child's perceptions that they should or should not use technology in their social network. But a child's positive affect about using the technology and their perception of how useful it is are the key drivers in them using the technology. Their friends affect their attitudes and their use, but parental influence is still significant.

Authoritative vs. Permissive Parenting in the Digital Age

On the opposite end of the scale are permissive parents. They respond to their teens' wishes and indulge their demands. The problem with this would-be empathetic approach is that it allows too much freedom for the teen without demanding responsibility. It's hard for any teen – no matter how careful – to navigate today's technological landscape without getting into trouble unless they are given parameters and rules. Online flak takes many forms and parents need to help kids fend off every one of them. At a minimum, parents can make sure their home computer runs good virus protection, spyware blockers, and a firewall. This alone will prevent some of the problems that bedevil Internet explorers of all ages.

When it comes to parenting styles, experts often talk about them in terms of two factors: parental responsiveness and parental demandingness. Authoritative parents are both highly responsive and demanding. They know where their teens are and whom they're with. They keep tabs on their kids without being obtrusive. The parents of teens who develop an allegiance to higher principles are usually parents who are keen to listen to their kids, but who also hold them accountable. Guidelines are established and kids are expected to have strict curfews. Parents of cyberkids need to show even more authority if they're to steer their tech-savvy offspring toward ethical technological choices. Parents can have the best of both worlds by establishing ground rules even as they ensure their kids have plenty of technological freedom. Put another way: parents need to be both helicopter and stealth bombers. They need both to hover and to surprise.

Adapting Parenting Styles to Technology Trends

The article is divided into two parts: Part I considers the historical evidence on the links between societal changes and parenting and the implications it may hold for our current world. Part II reviews the existing evidence about how children and parents use technology and the emerging lessons from the scientific literature on parenting. It describes some challenges and considerations that we consider when we explore how to adapt traditional parenting concepts and behaviors to this new and increasingly technological world. Specifically, will the traditional ideas about what is optimal parenting suffice in an age that is characterized by increasing digital interconnectedness? What are the best ways to prepare kids for their 22nd-century world? The myriad changes that characterize our current world motivate us to pursue these questions in the spirit of understanding how to ensure our kids are well-prepared for tomorrow.

Just as many popular theories about the effects of technology on family life assume a traditional family and home, they also seem to imply that traditional parenting styles and behaviors are effective and appropriate in a world characterized by technology. However, with the ready availability of research-based guidelines for optimal parenting behavior, it is increasingly less necessary to rely on intuition rather than science when raising children. These insights come from the fields of psychology or human development, largely focusing on the existence of optimal parenting styles that are associated with the best outcomes in children. They show that parents who are both responsive and demanding are more likely to have children who are competent. Many who study children and families have recently begun considering the science of parenting in the digital world and asking whether fundamental ideas about how to be a good parent need to change.

CHAPTER 12

Cultural and Socioeconomic Factors in Digital Pare

Regardless of parent perceived benefits of television and gaming, the American Academy of Associations recommends that parents avoid all television for children under the age of two, regardless of whether the program is perceived as educational, fearing that children may not develop skills that only play can provide. In addition, because of the vulnerability of children under two's ability to process video content, parents must be aware of their preschooler's television and gaming use, since parents should watch these shows and games with their children to help discuss, interpret, and understand content. Since families will continue to use television and gaming as a way to keep children occupied and entertained after the school day has ended, parents of older children should allow a maximum of two hours of combined television and gaming time, 1/3 hours of 0-6 hour time should be high-quality programming. However, despite minimum level recommendations on the "commercial advertisement" during television and multimedia use in the lives of American children, many preschoolers are using cell phones, computers, and video games.

From Some Leeway for Parents, 2005/2006 – A study on how much television and computer use children under two years old are exposed to, the American Academy of Pediatrics concluded that parents allow television and computer use based on cultural and socioeconomic factors. Parents of low-income children are more likely to view television and computer games as beneficial to learning and development; pressure to own computers in order to help children catch up with technology-driven society influences the amount of television used, parents' decision to limit television, and purchase of computer games; and parents may feel that participation in electronic media improves academic readiness. Only half of parents of children under two years of age realize it is best not to allow television to be viewed at this young age. For middle-income parents, the conclusion was that watching television and playing computer games was used to keep children entertained when parents were busy, bought software that was designed to be educational but was not always educational, pressured by society to use computers at a young age, and used television to captivate any time that was otherwise "wasted" by parents. Middle-income parents report that programs aired on public broadcasting television networks are positively educational and allow their three-year-olds to view up to two hours of shows such as "Sesame Street", "Dora the Explorer", "Blues Clues", and "Bob the Builder" per day.

Impact of Cultural Norms on Technology Use in Families
American homes have come to enjoy a wide variety of technological advances. These take many different forms that can break out into five categories. These categories underscore the ways in which technology has become deeply integrated into everyday life. Access technology relates to needing and wanting internet access. Mobile devices and wireless networks have proliferated through all levels

of society. Educational technology is profoundly impacting schools and students. Work technology is often brought home, where complete separation between work and home life is nearly impossible. Finally, entertainment technology is deeply implicated in couch time and family bonding. These technologies primarily serve parents' everyday needs, whether individual ones or those as part of a family unit. In all of these categories, parents face difficult choices about how and why to incorporate the technology. This often means negotiating family use of technology based on a different organizing principle—such as happiness, fairness, or well-being—that prioritizes their commitment to their child.

Most Americans have a strong belief in the power of technology to move society forward. Despite mounting evidence to the contrary, we have a steadfast belief that the internet is an unmitigated public good. This cultural heritage is combined with an American sense of moral superiority. Alongside an almost idolatrous embrace of technology and tools is an entrenched resistance to any critique. These cultural norms shape people's understanding of the value of technology and their willingness to forego the outcomes that they produce. It's very risky to question the role of technology in everyday life. This leads to a culture where families are basically caught between three dueling narratives. One asserts that technology will save the world. One asserts that technology is ruining everything. One asserts that people are powerless to resist the advent of new technologies. All of these positions are extreme, and they're all unproductive for parents facing challenging decisions about how to integrate technology into their family life.

Addressing the Digital Divide and Access Disparities
This increased awareness and response did not address the digital divide challenges that have been ongoing and will continue to exist.

A good start is to understand that solutions are unique to local situations and that technology must provide equitable and innovative solutions. Buildings can be internet hotspots for entire neighborhoods, with earth-friendly lower energy costs. High-speed connections would immediately provide important functions to support the community in times of crisis or lessened levels of connected learning, facilitating online learning, professional development, and tele-health care. Community access resources could create job opportunities while nurturing strong lifelong learners while hardware and free or affordable service can provide simple, immediate solutions. Providing computer ownership and access is necessary to developing digital fluency and readiness for our students' future competitiveness in college and their careers, but the recognition of all online needs is critical in determining realistic feasibility. Information literacy is another important factor in decreasing the digital divide. An educated community is a better community. Providing help for our students as they learn to judge the quality of information they come across is essential. Libraries could offer a monthly technology class for their patrons, which includes widely used websites and online technology literacy skills. Community access to qualified and knowledgeable resources could include technology aides, who could have the important responsibility of teaching different and innovative ways to communicate and access information and resources, thus shrinking the digital divide.

The digital divide plays a significant role with many parents and their technology acumen as well as their access to devices and the internet. And families at all income levels are experiencing the same screen-time struggles. Limited access to interactive media and the internet can also adversely affect a child's vocabulary development. Connecting with others is as important for kids as it is for adults, and digital connectivity is equally important to both. So what is the solution? Many tech companies talk about how they are addressing the digital divide, providing hardware and affordable service for internet access. A recent example of this solution can be found in the news. Companies like T-Mobile, Sprint, Windstream, and Charter Communications offered increased data allowances, wireless hotspots, and free service to students in low-income families so that children could do their school work from home during the COVID-19 pandemic when schools were closed.

CHAPTER 13

Parental Self-Care and Digital Well-Being

This chapter argues that good digital parenting begins with good digital self-care, and that nurturing parents, in fact, need to be nurtured. It then considers how to practice and maintain shared family values online and offline, and the importance of focusing on memories as well as moments. Finally, it offers and considers advice, in the form of "Digital You and Mini You Weekly Reflections," for the parent interested in nurturing both yourself and your child and who is eager to encourage the development of a more vibrant digital family-life balance.

Given the importance of parental well-being in fostering and maintaining healthy family relationships, especially in the digital context, it may seem paradoxical that, as parents, we often overlook our own barriers to digital well-being. We tend to think of digital parenting experts as helping us ensure that our children lead fulfilling and rewarding lives in our fast-paced, digital society, or as advising us on how to limit their screen time to help protect them from the perils that lurk beyond the family firewall. We rarely focus on the fact that we, as parents, often struggle to achieve our own digital well-being and life balance or to engage our whole selves with our children when our own digital distractions are competing for our time and attention.

Setting Healthy Boundaries for Parental Tech Use

Nurse Marcie encourages parents to "put your phone in your pocket, not your child's and not yours. This needs to be a two-way street. Pay attention to your child, be present and responsive, and role model the behavior you want your child to learn." Deborah with Pi'co advises parents to "set times of the day where you are not contactable via your devices so you can focus on our children." And Magdalena with Ibulb explains that "parent/child moments are unique and absolutely necessary for a healthy communication between you and your child. If you are with your child and try to answer a call or text, explain what you are doing quickly and kindly." Make it clear until what moment they will have your undivided attention. Their interest cup will be full and they will allow you to finish your talk.

A second technology-related issue many parents of young children are contending with is the impact of their own use of tablets and smartphones. "An increasing number of mothers and fathers are finding that good old-fashioned parenting—where you play and chat with your children at the playground or craft build with them on the kitchen floor—is being replaced by tablet, smartphone, and social media use." According to Alessandra, "when adults tune out of family life with the click of a button, it's the children who are left to pay the price." Hence, it can be difficult to set appropriate tech boundaries for the little ones when we ourselves don't know where to draw the line! Ginelle with Playful Bee encourages parents to "think about this: what does it feel like when you are trying to have a conversation with someone who is consistently checking their phone? It makes you feel unimportant and not engaged." This is not a message parents want to send to their babies or toddlers.

Practicing Mindfulness and Digital Detox
Sensitive and consistent response by caregivers fosters secure attachment. But the near continuous access to digital devices may prevent kids from being able to use such cues to create a secure attachment. Kids' absorption in digital activities interferes with parents' and kids' opportunities to respond to one another's bids for shared visual attention - which in real-world environments fosters social and linguistic growth. In fact, the mere presence of a cell phone between parent and child during a toy-free play session reduces the extent and quality of the verbal and nonverbal interaction between the two. When teaching parents to respond contingently to key alerts and social bids of their infants, enabling their children to feel soothed when distressed, and fostering a secure attachment, cell phones do not belong and teachers' delicate and sensitive work was also constrained by the presence of cell phones. The goal here is not to blame parents, teachers, or caregivers. Cell phones are helpful devices and at times necessary in the life of busy parents, working mothers, and teachers. But the goal is to encourage all of us to be as mindful as possible about when and where we use our cell phones for the sake of children and students.

Getting engaged in mindfulness - being present in the here and now - is of utmost necessity when living in this digital era. Achieving balance, regulating our inner selves, and focusing on the moment is key to achieving optimal mental and emotional well-being. Mindfulness influences the interaction between the brain, mind, body, and behavior in ways that can enhance our kids' lives and lead to more effective functioning in education, work, and relationships. It's equally important for kids as it is for parents, guardians, and teachers. Unfortunately, kids' exposure to and engagement with all aspects of their environment occurs almost continually, with most days filled with movement from one activity or structure to another. Thus, they have little opportunity to be fully aware of what is going on around them.

CHAPTER 14

The Future of Parenting in a Tech-Driven World

We suspect that in a generation, we will know much more about what our children's intense engagement with technology is doing to their brains, their bodies, and their emotional well-being. We suspect that technology developers and marketers will have become partners in helping all of us mold our children's digital lives in directions that are good and sound for the whole child. On many levels and in many ways, our children's lives will look very different from those of our own childhoods. But our job in helping our children to find and reach toward their full potential will not really have changed all that much. The goals of parenting – to grow in wisdom, to act with and cultivate compassion, to make use of one's intelligence and talents, to be both self-motivated and group-oriented, to possess and practice self-discipline, and – also very much a goal – to seek personal happiness – do not change.

Welcome to the paradox of parenting in an era of expanding screens: encouraging and overseeing our children's use of technology is imperative for their healthy development, but resisting that same technology and teaching their hearts and minds to function the old-fashioned way remains, in many respects, our most crucial task as parents and educators. We hope that this book has given you a fuller understanding of both of those related challenges.

Emerging Technologies and Their Potential Impact on Parenting
Emerging technologies and more precisely the digital integration and new applications of so-called known technologies are offering more and more novel tools and gadgets that are used or will soon be used in the life of adults but also in the lives of their young ones. Our ability to accurately predict how the rapid advancement and integration of new and known technologies will shape aspects of society is important. A lack of such knowledge will inevitably affect the maturation of these emerging technologies, as well as the discussions about whether they are heading in an acceptable direction and how they may be influencing people. Aware of the constantly emerging technologies and applications in Ed Tech, we have entered an era where custom systems can be developed in education in order to shape the changes and therefore affect progress in this important and always-evolving domain.

This chapter highlights emerging and soon to emerge technologies and their potential impact on parenting in the digital age. The prediction of the possible consequences of such technologies helps in their potential development and surveillance in order to converge to acceptable standards and designs, rather than following paths that one is reigning in out of necessity. The age of exascale machines is upon us and the combination of big data coming from thousands of sources and the parallel capability of novel big data analytics means the development of more and extremely informative systems. Such personalized parenting systems will have tremendous potential to change or deform the way kids grow up. The chapter also highlights safeguards of these technologies, raising concerns about the reliability of these technologies and important societal repercussions if the data on which they are based are imprecise and biased.

Preparing Children for a Tech-Integrated Future
Role modeling and take-your-child-to-work programming can provide a limited platform for children's care before they naturally integrate the tools so prevalent in your work world. Ultimately, the tech generation will be successful as well-meaning global citizens if they are nurtured by those closest to them to use technology in collaborative and mindful ways, to differentiate relevant signals from all the digital noise. Just as the preceding and ongoing science generation was in part the product of a multi-generational effort that culminated in science being a societal value, the tech generation can be nurtured to grow out of the house where parents have prepared the concrete foundations for success.

The digital revolution has caused the most recent shift in human development since the Industrial Revolution. Digital tools pervade every area of our lives and, at a pace that is ever accelerating, are becoming ever more deeply embedded in culture. As the tech generation, preparing children for this tech-driven world is, in part, preparing them for the world in which they find themselves. This is an important role for parents to play in guiding children through the transition into being thoughtful and productive digital citizens. Whether it is choosing the right games or enabling online learning, interested and involved parents can play a strong role in the integration of digital technologies into children's lives. As a parent accepting guidance from those children means adding technological help to parenting tools.

CHAPTER 15

CHAPTER 16

Conclusion and Key Takeaways

These are the principles and rules of parenting in the digital age that have emerged out of the discussions and various reports covered in the book. Many come from our own thoughts on the topic; others have been adapted and modified from the various positions in debates. It should be noted that the discussions have tended to look at the various situations in the developed world but these will apply to poorer communities and to the developing countries as and when technology use becomes more widespread.

1. Being a parent is a never-ending, 24-hour, lifelong job which comes with no instructions. But in a society that is characterized by rapid change with respect to technology, it is unrealistic and indeed hostile to parents to suggest or expect that they should have the time or capability to be at the forefront of their understanding of developments in the parenting of children and young people and to understand the several new landscapes of learning, from the digital playground to the social networking space.

2. Although kids are often streets ahead of their parents with respect to digital technology, their moral compasses and general wellbeing are not. That is why decisions about how children and young

people should regulate their internet usage and the appropriateness or otherwise of the various applications and tools of social networking are best taken within the family. The challenge for governments is to support families in that process, providing suitable guidance and rules, leaving open the themes of consent and peer pressure, learning about different cultural approaches, and the relative impacts on the child online and in the physical world.

Summary of Key Points Discussed in the Book

At its heart, this book encourages carers to be confident, clear, involved, and proactive regarding their digital kids. Provided potential pitfalls are recognized and managed, digital technologies offer significant potential to help young people develop into happy, healthy, and balanced adults. This book is specifically targeted at families but will also be helpful to school staff, pediatricians, psychologists, social workers, and public health practitioners. Additionally, the book offers an introduction to key terms and concepts for researchers and reviews popular therapies designed to address problematic digital consumption.

The book Parenting in the Digital Age provides an overview of the key issues associated with digital kids and presents a range of strategies and solutions that will help safeguard children in a digital world. While there is a high level of anxiety and confusion surrounding how to best raise children in the digital age, this book is also designed to provide reassurance to parents and carers. Within this book, misconceptions and misunderstandings regarding digital kids are identified and clarified, along with specific issues which require attention and moderation, including the potential for problematic digital consumption to develop into tech addiction.

www.ingramcontent.com/pod-product-compliance
Lightning Source LLC
LaVergne TN
LVHW042252070526
838201LV00104B/295